TRUE ANIMAL RESCUES

RESCUED
by a
HORSE

by Joyce Markovics

CHERRY LAKE PRESS
Ann Arbor, Michigan

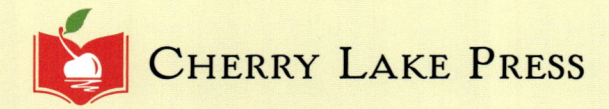

CHERRY LAKE PRESS

Published in the United States of America by Cherry Lake Publishing
Ann Arbor, Michigan
www.cherrylakepublishing.com

Reading Adviser: Beth Walker Gambro, MS Ed., Reading Consultant, Yorkville, IL

Book Designer: Ed Morgan
Book Developer: Bowerbird Books

Photo Credits: freepik.com, cover, title page, and table of contents; © Sari ONeal/Shutterstock, 4–5; © Rita_Kochmarjova/Shutterstock, 6; © Mircea Costina/Shutterstock, 7; Courtesy of Kimberly Stargatt, 8, 9; freepik.com, 10–11, 12–13, 14–15; © Fairfax Photo.com, 16–17; © Caftor/Shutterstock, 18; © William Edge/Shutterstock, 19; © OryPhotography/Shutterstock, 20–21.

Library of Congress Cataloging-in-Publication Data has been filed and is available at catalog.loc.gov.

Printed in the United States of America

Note from publisher: Websites change regularly, and their future contents are outside of our control. Supervise children when conducting any recommended online searches for extended learning opportunities.

Contents

Heroic Horses

It was an average day on Robert Bennington's ranch. He walked to the **paddock** and called his four horses. They usually came running. But this day, they didn't. *How odd*, Robert thought. Then, in the distance, Robert spotted several extra-furry dogs.

After Robert got a better look, he was shocked. The "dogs" were, in fact, a pack of coyotes. And they were running toward the rancher. "I called out to my horse," Robert said. "Scottee, get by Daddy fast!" What happened next stunned Robert.

Horses have a great sense of smell. They can often smell enemies, such as coyotes and wolves, from far away.

The coyotes slowed down and crept closer. Scottee and the other horses **galloped** toward Robert. They formed a circle around him. One of the coyotes **lunged** at Robert's horse, Danny Boy. The horse fought back. He kicked the snarling animal.

A horse kick is powerful enough to break bone.

Another coyote attacked. Scottee kicked and stomped it. "The coyote started whining," said Robert. Finally, the pack ran off. "All I can remember after is resting my head on Scottee and crying," Robert said. "They saved my life." Robert will always be thankful for his hero horses.

Coyotes live together in packs of up to 7 adults.

Phoebe and Kimberly

Robert believes the bond between humans and horses is strong. Kimberly Stargatt feels this way too. She and her **mare** Phoebe have a very close relationship. "Her soul has an energy that matches, and gives back to, mine," said Kimberly.

Kimberly and Phoebe

One day, Kimberly was riding Phoebe in a jumping **competition**. As they were approaching a wall, Phoebe hesitated. "I flew over the wall and landed on my back," said Kimberly. Then she looked up and saw Phoebe flying over the wall too. "And the only place to land was on me," Kimberly recalled.

Kimberly and Phoebe jumping over a fence during a competition

Show jumping is a sport where riders jump their horses over a series of fences and walls.

A terrified Kimberly **braced** for impact. "I felt the pressure of her hoof over my heart," she remembers. "I just closed my eyes and waited for the end." Amazingly, Phoebe shifted her weight midair. The horse fell backward into the wall.

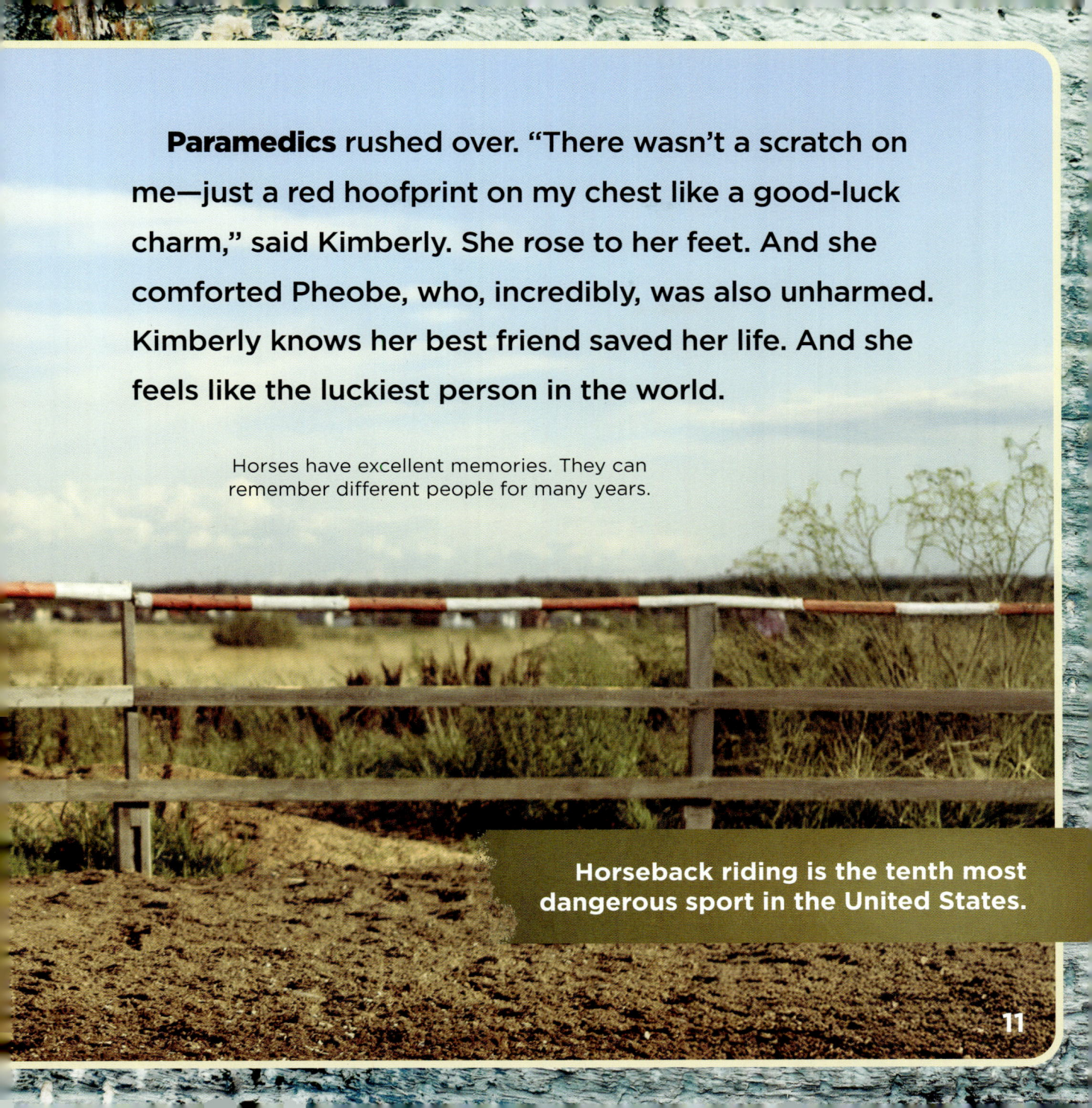

Paramedics rushed over. "There wasn't a scratch on me—just a red hoofprint on my chest like a good-luck charm," said Kimberly. She rose to her feet. And she comforted Pheobe, who, incredibly, was also unharmed. Kimberly knows her best friend saved her life. And she feels like the luckiest person in the world.

Horses have excellent memories. They can remember different people for many years.

Horseback riding is the tenth most dangerous sport in the United States.

Jeune the Lifesaver

Anthony Sexton also feels lucky. And his horse, Jeune Mark, is the reason why. Anthony was home in Australia with Jeune. They were watching a wildfire in the mountains. "We thought we were safe," he recalls. Then, suddenly, the sky darkened and it got cool and smoky. "We're in trouble," said Anthony. Pretty soon, there was fire everywhere. Anthony **mounted** Jeune, hoping to escape the flames.

Horses have an outstanding sense of smell. They can sniff out wildfires and other dangers.

Anthony and Jeune looked for a way out. The horse trotted down a road. "But the fire came up behind us," Anthony said. He thought to himself, *That's it. This is where I'm going to die.* Then Jeune did something **astonishing**.

Under the right conditons, wildfires can double in size within minutes.

The horse **bucked**, sending Anthony over a **guardrail**. Steps away was a creek. Anthony slid into the water. He stayed there until the flames died down. Then he followed the creek home. Anthony worried that Jeune had **perished** in the fire.

15

Anthony kisses Jeune Mark. The horse survived the fire with burns around his eyes and nose, which healed over time.

Once home, "everything was gone," said Anthony. His home was destroyed. But there in the paddock was his hero Jeune Mark! "I was over the moon," Anthony remembers. "I honestly thought he was going to be dead." The horse had run through a maze of fire and lived. If it weren't for Jeune, Anthony knows he might not have survived.

The deadly blaze killed nine people. The night after the fire, Anthony slept next to Jeune Mark.

17

Kerry to the Rescue

Like Jeune Mark, Kerry the horse saved her owner's life. One afternoon, Fiona Boyd was on her farm in Scotland. She was leading a calf into the barn. Out of nowhere, the calf's mother charged her. The mother cow knocked Fiona over. Then it trampled her.

"Every time I tried to crawl away, the cow just slammed me again," Fiona said. "I was absolutely terrified. Nobody was there to help me." Fiona rolled into a ball to protect her head. As she did, she worried that other cows might join the attack.

The mother cow likely attacked Fiona because she thought her baby was in danger.

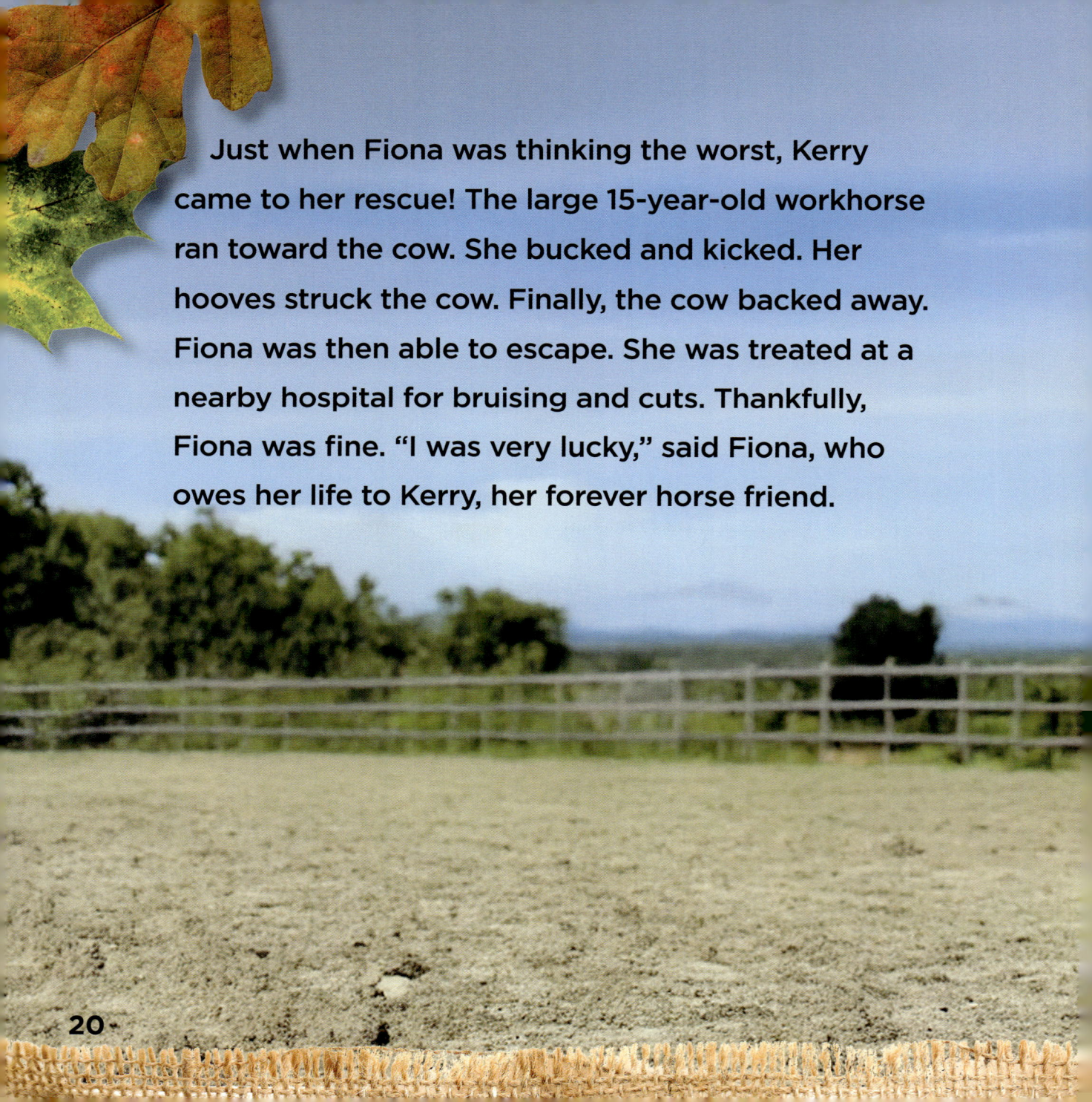

Just when Fiona was thinking the worst, Kerry came to her rescue! The large 15-year-old workhorse ran toward the cow. She bucked and kicked. Her hooves struck the cow. Finally, the cow backed away. Fiona was then able to escape. She was treated at a nearby hospital for bruising and cuts. Thankfully, Fiona was fine. "I was very lucky," said Fiona, who owes her life to Kerry, her forever horse friend.

When a horse bucks, it can seriously hurt an animal or person.

21

PROFILE:
Horse Rescuers

Why do some horses rescue and protect people? Here are some amazing horse qualities that could explain why.

Loyal

Horses form deep bonds with humans. They can remember individuals, especially kind ones, for years or even decades!

Affectionate

While horses aren't affectionate in the same way as humans, they "love" us by seeking our company. They will follow and lick people they like and trust.

Sensitive

Horses are sensitive to our emotions. They can tell when someone is sad or stressed and help them. This is why horses are often used as therapy animals.

Glossary

astonishing (uh-STON-ish-ing)
amazing

braced (BRAYST)
prepared oneself for something unpleasant

bucked (BUHKT)
when a horse jumped and kicked out its back legs

competition (kom-puh-TISH-uhn)
a contest of some kind

galloped (GAL-uhpt)
ran at a very fast speed

guardrail (GARD-rail)
a rail that is used for protection, such as one along the side of a highway

lunged (LUHNJD)
moved forward quickly and suddenly

mare (MAIR)
a female horse

mounted (MOUNT-id)
climbed on a horse

paddock (PAD-uhk)
an enclosed field for horses or other animals

paramedics (pair-uh-MED-iks)
medical workers who ride in ambulances and give life-saving first aid

perished (PAIR-ishd)
died

Find Out More

BOOKS

125 Animals That Changed the World. Washington, DC: National Geographic Kids, 2019.

Markovics, Joyce. *Champs! Inspirational Animals: Hero Horses*. Ann Arbor, MI: Cherry Lake Press, 2024.

Recio, Belinda. *When Animals Rescue*. New York, NY: Skyhorse Publishing, 2021.

WEBSITES

Explore these online sources with an adult:

BC SPCA: 10 Fun Facts About Horses

Britannica Kids: Horse

National Geographic: Horse

Index

About the Author

Joyce Markovics is drawn to stories that tug at her heart. When she's not writing books for kids, she volunteers at an animal sanctuary where dozens of different species peacefully coexist. Joyce dedicates this book to the memory of Phoebe and would like to thank Kimberly Stargatt for being a part of this project.